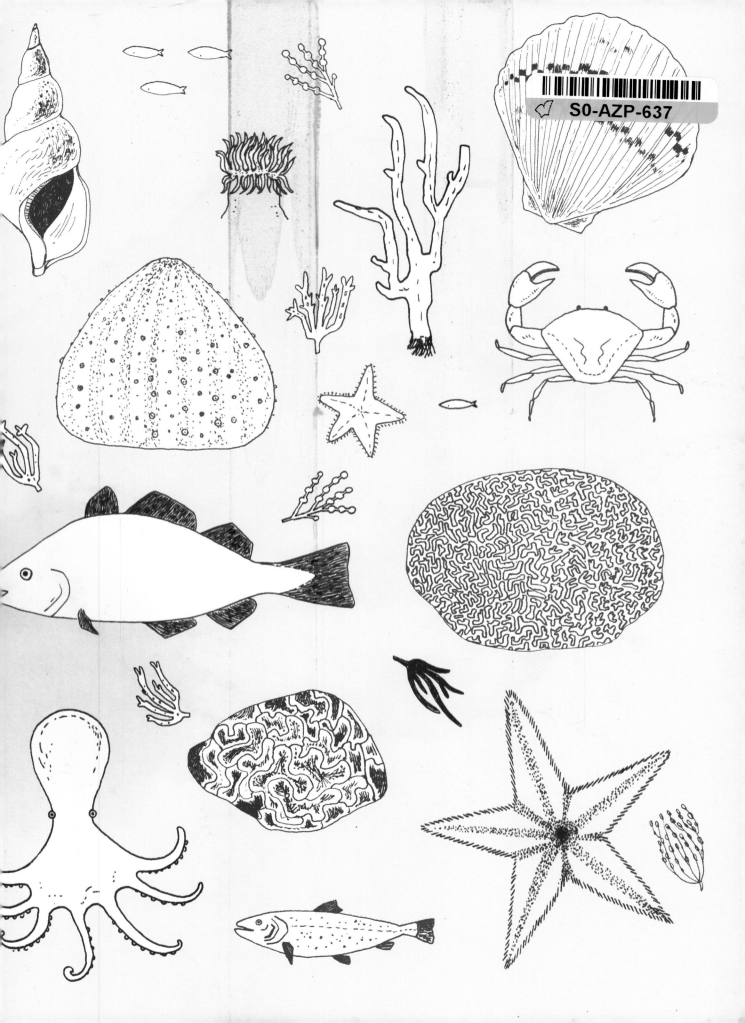

Drawing in the Sea

Hello and welcome to Drawing in the Sea. Before we get started, here are some interesting facts about the sea.

The sea is very, very important. Around 70 percent of the earth is covered by water; much of this is seawater.

Also, around 70 percent of the human body is made up of water (but not seawater)!

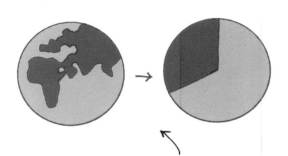

If all the sea and all the land were put together in big lumps, the globe would look something like this.

The main oceans of the world are:

The largest of these is the Pacific Ocean.

The Pacific Ocean

The Atlantic Ocean

The Southern Ocean

The Arctic Ocean

The Indian Ocean

You cannot drink water from the sea because it is full of salt.

Salt

—ughh

The sea was formed many years ago...

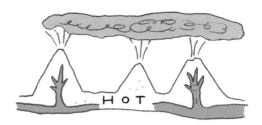

As the hot earth cooled, volcanoes erupted and produced a mixture of gases, including hydrogen and oxygen.

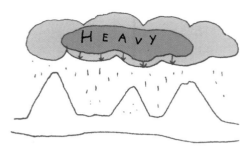

The atmosphere became so heavy with water vapor that the water fell as rain.

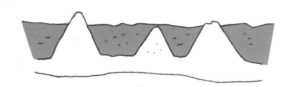

Eventually, the earth cooled and the oceans were formed.

There are huge mountains and rugged landscapes beneath the ocean.

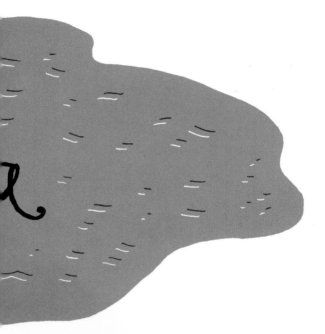

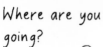

I'm going to climb the mountains in the sea.

Where are you going?

?

There are plenty of fish in the sea - and also many other creatures...

OK, that's enough of that. Let's draw!

What did these fish eat for dinner? Draw it.

Spaghetti

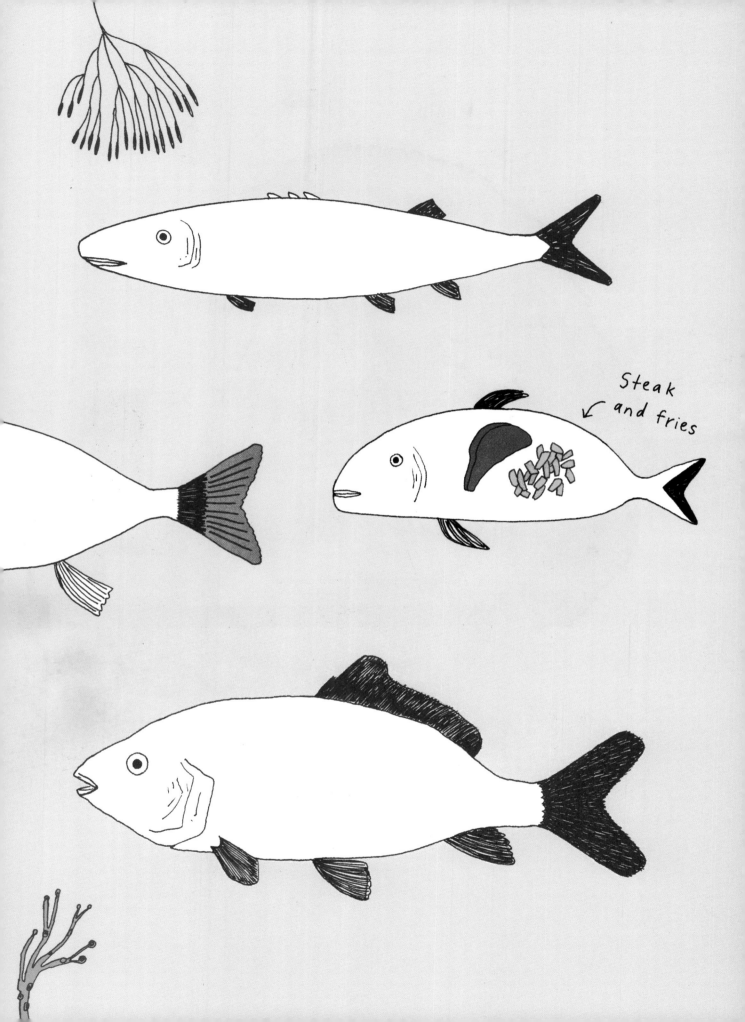

Steak and fries

Who is traveling on the ship? Draw some faces looking out of the portholes.

What Color is the Sea?

Blue

Sea colored

Bluey-green

Greeny-blue

Green

Turquoise

Brown

Gray

Pink

Azure

What color is the sea?

The sea's color reflects the sky, therefore it often appears blue.
But depending on the light, and sometimes other things such as algae
and plant life, the sea can appear green, gray, turquoise, or brown.

Color these seas.

What color is the sea at sunset?

What color is a frozen sea?

What color is the sea at night?

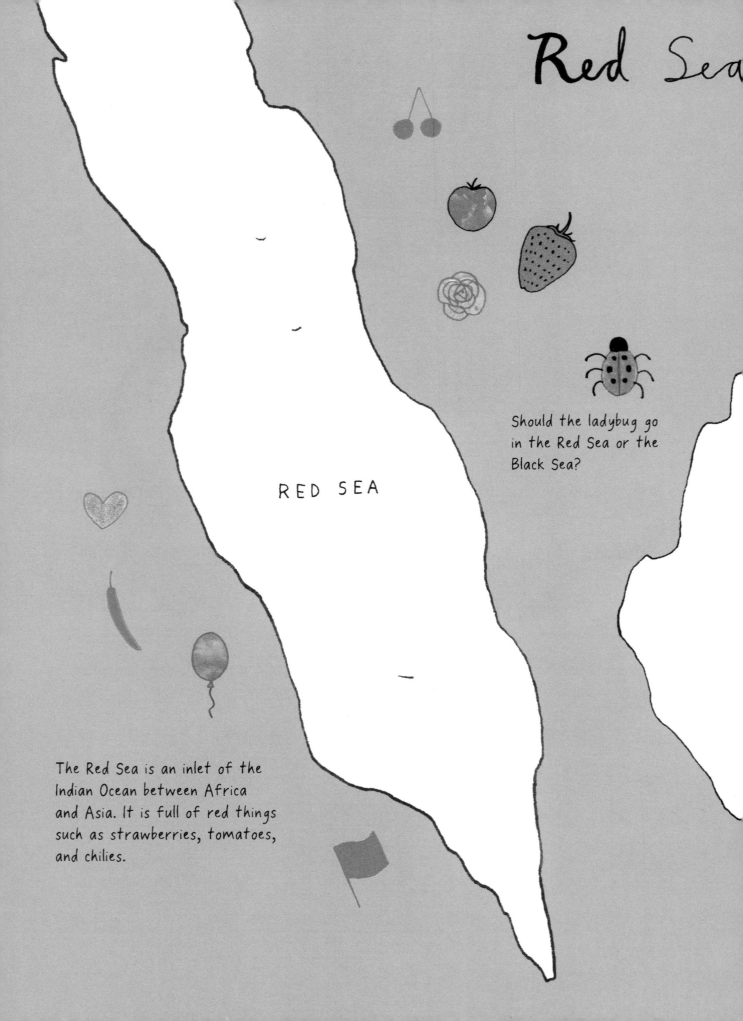

RED SEA

Should the ladybug go in the Red Sea or the Black Sea?

The Red Sea is an inlet of the Indian Ocean between Africa and Asia. It is full of red things such as strawberries, tomatoes, and chilies.

and Black Sea

The Black Sea is bordered by Romania, Turkey, Russia, and several other countries. It is full of black things like ink, blackbirds, and beetles.

BLACK SEA

Draw some red things in the Red Sea and some black things in the Black Sea!

Ship in a bottle

Large bottle or small ship? This ship is far too large to fit in this bottle.

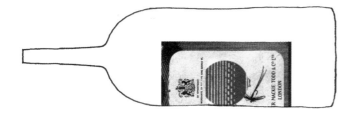

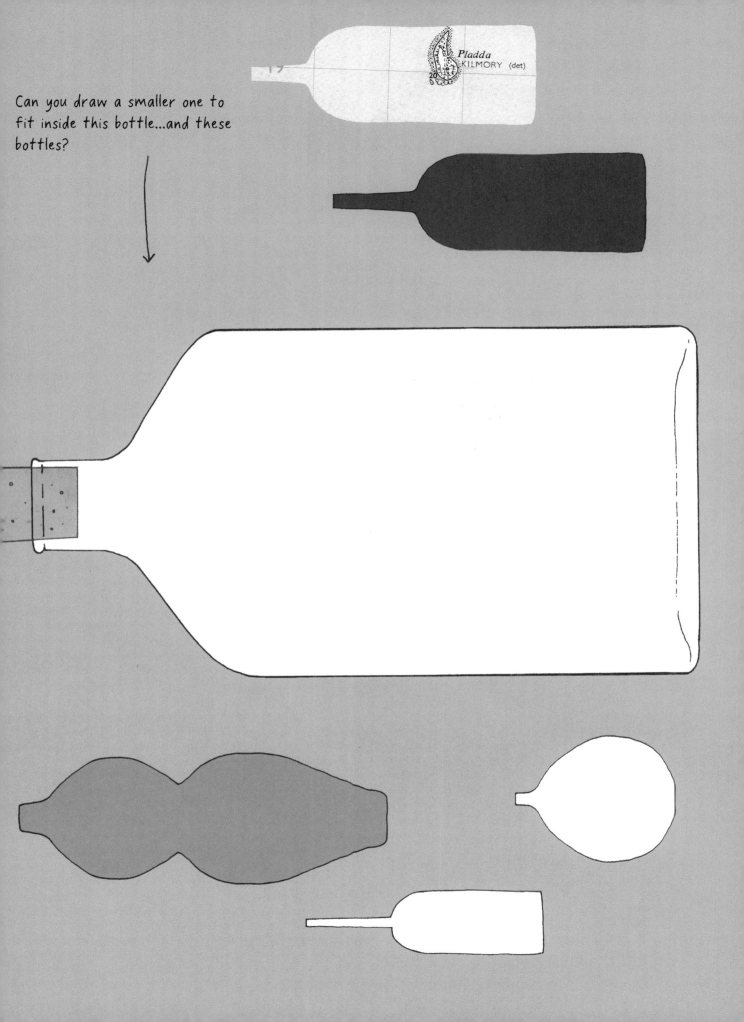

Can you draw a smaller one to fit inside this bottle...and these bottles?

Decorate these salty seafarers with lots of tattoos.

TATT

Draw a parrot on this man's shoulder!

LARGE and Small

The sea is home to over 20,000 species of fish and millions of other plants and animals. The largest of these is the blue whale, which can grow to 98 feet in length and weigh 210 tons!

The blue whale is even bigger than the world's largest dinosaur!

Its heart can weigh as much as a car and its tongue as much as an elephant!

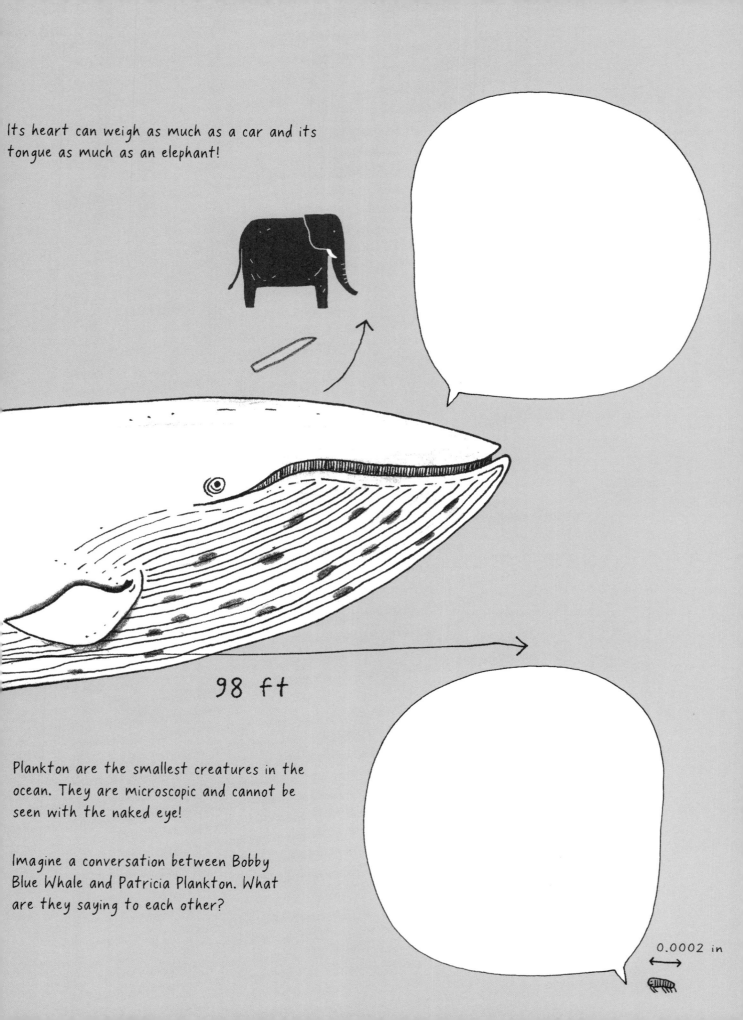

98 ft

Plankton are the smallest creatures in the ocean. They are microscopic and cannot be seen with the naked eye!

Imagine a conversation between Bobby Blue Whale and Patricia Plankton. What are they saying to each other?

0.0002 in

Salt

Why is the sea full of salt?
As rocks are worn down by the sea, small amounts of salts are released into the water flowing over and through the rocks. Salt does not evaporate, so it stays in the ocean.

Draw some salt in the sea.

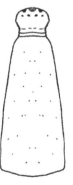

Now, draw some sea in the salt.

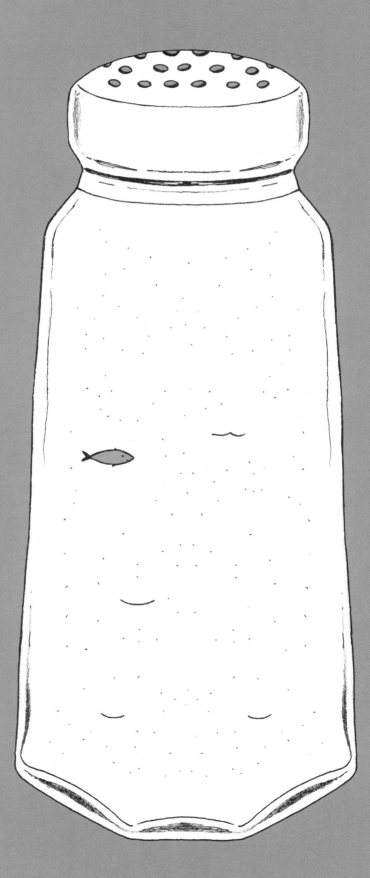

the Dead Sea

The Dead Sea is the lowest point on earth!

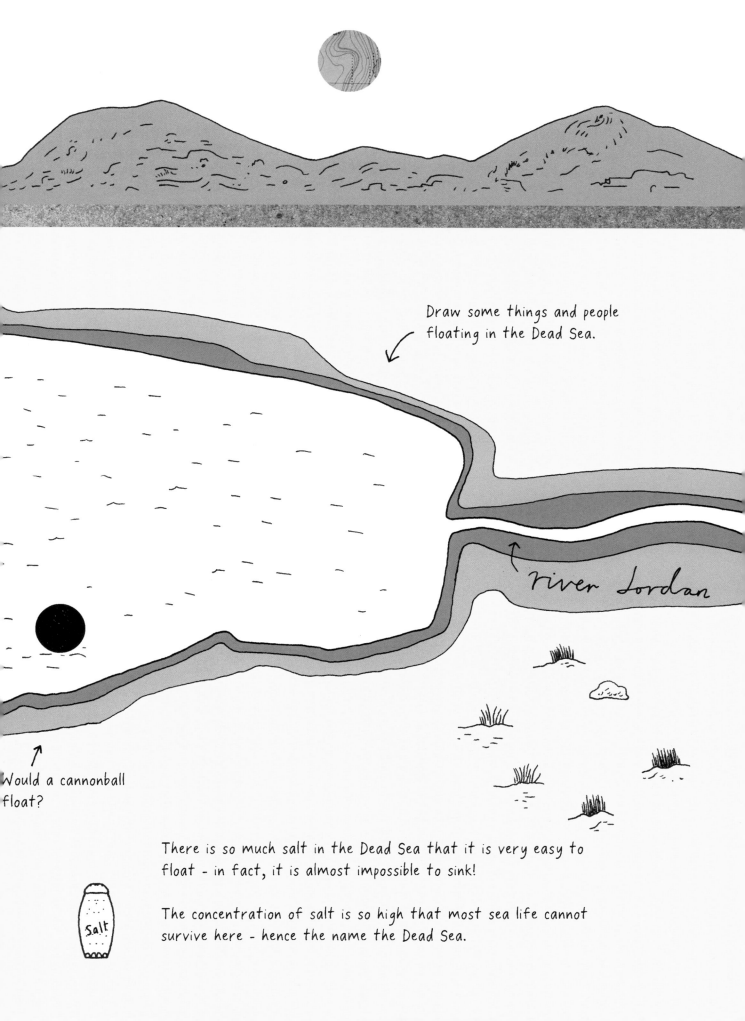

Draw some things and people floating in the Dead Sea.

river Jordan

Would a cannonball float?

There is so much salt in the Dead Sea that it is very easy to float - in fact, it is almost impossible to sink!

The concentration of salt is so high that most sea life cannot survive here - hence the name the Dead Sea.

Salt

These fishermen have gotten themselves very tangled up. Who has caught what?
Follow the lines to find out.

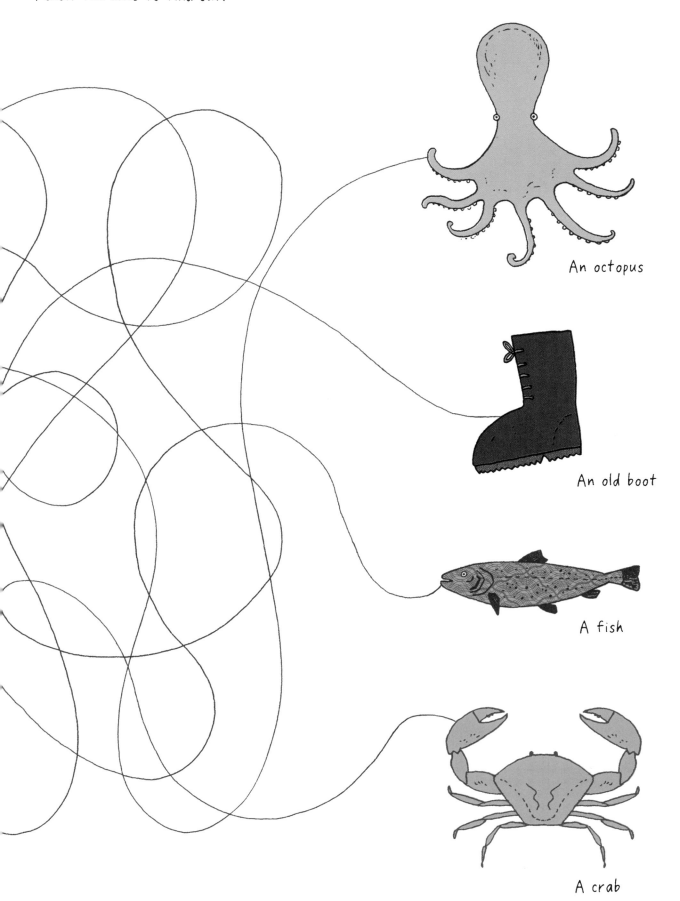

An octopus

An old boot

A fish

A crab

Shells

Sometimes people say that it is possible to hear the sound of the ocean coming from a seashell.

Imagine what you can hear coming from these shells. Draw it!

Different boats...

There are many weird and wonderful vessels to be found at sea. Here are a few. Match the picture to the name...

Viking longship

Chinese "junk"

Pirate ship

Cargo ship

Bathtub

Kayak

Colander!?

Banana boat

Yellow submarine

Rock Pools

As the tide moves out, pools of seawater are left in the rocks. These are full of life - limpets, crabs, starfish, sea anemones, seaweed, and much more!

Draw some sea creatures in these rock pools.

A sea anemone looks like a lump of jelly until it is under the water and all its tentacles open!

Limpets (snails and slugs) cling to the rocks for dear life! Their shells protect the soft body of the mollusk inside.

Starfish are also known as sea stars.

Seabirds

Why don't seabirds get wet? Do they drink saltwater?
Seabirds are specially adapted to the marine environment.

Special gland to filter excess salt out of seawater.

Waterproofing (a mixture of wax and fat that is secreted from the preening gland).

Some bird poo can be used as a fertilizer for plants!

Webbed feet for swimming/ paddling.

Guillemot

Cormorar

Puffin

Seagull

Draw some birds in the sky and on the rocks.

Noah's Ark

There is a great flood coming, so Noah is saving two of each animal on his ark. So far he only has one of each animal.

Can you draw a pair for each animal?

Draw Mrs. Noah!

The storm is raging and the ark is being tossed around on the rough ocean! The animals are feeling ill...Draw some more storm clouds and rain coming from the clouds.

Desert Island

Imagine you are going to be
stranded on a desert island, miles
away from anywhere.

What would you take with you? Draw it here...

Johnny and the Whale

Hi, I'm Johnny and I have been swallowed by a whale, help!
Can you help me find my way out?

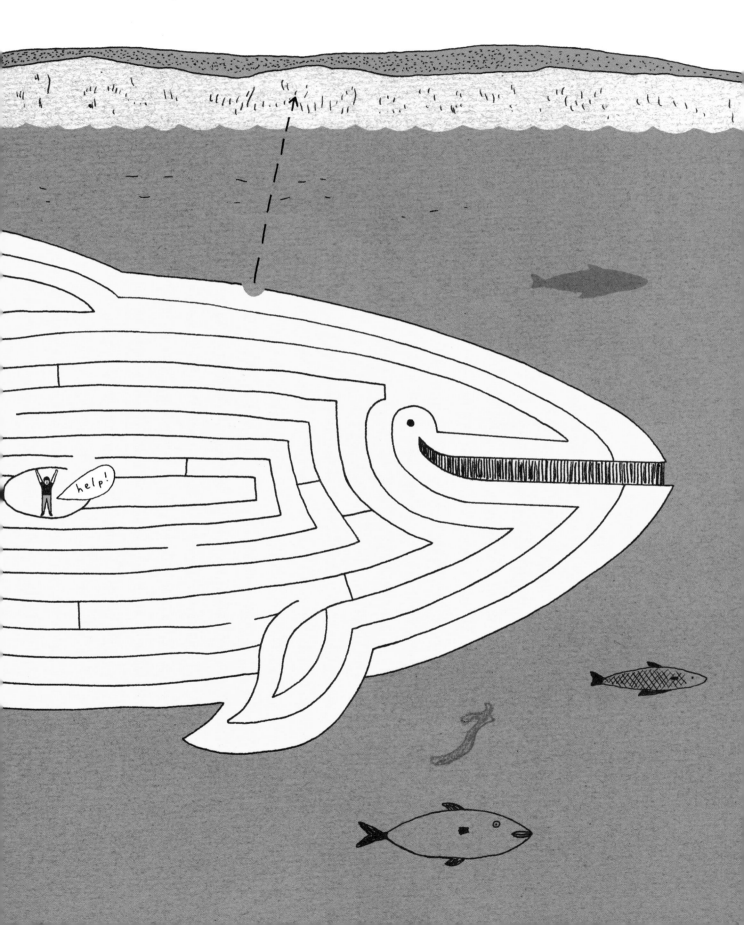

Breathing Underwater

How do fish breathe underwater?

Fish breathe in through their mouths and out through their gills. They absorb oxygen from the water through their gills.

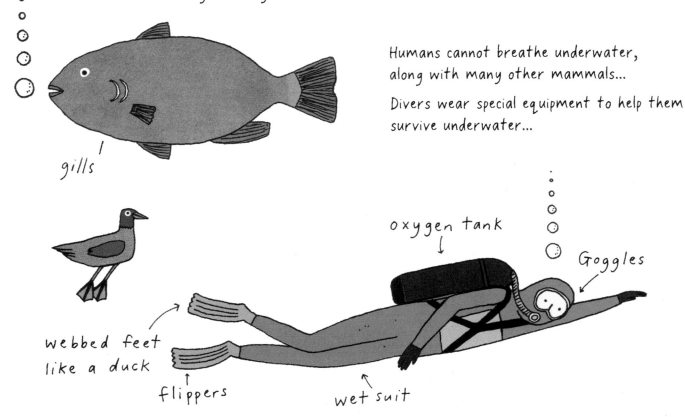

gills

Humans cannot breathe underwater, along with many other mammals...

Divers wear special equipment to help them survive underwater...

oxygen tank

Goggles

webbed feet like a duck

flippers

wet suit

This horse has grown scales, fins, and gills so now he can live in the sea!

Can you make these land creatures into sea creatures by giving them scales, fins, and gills?

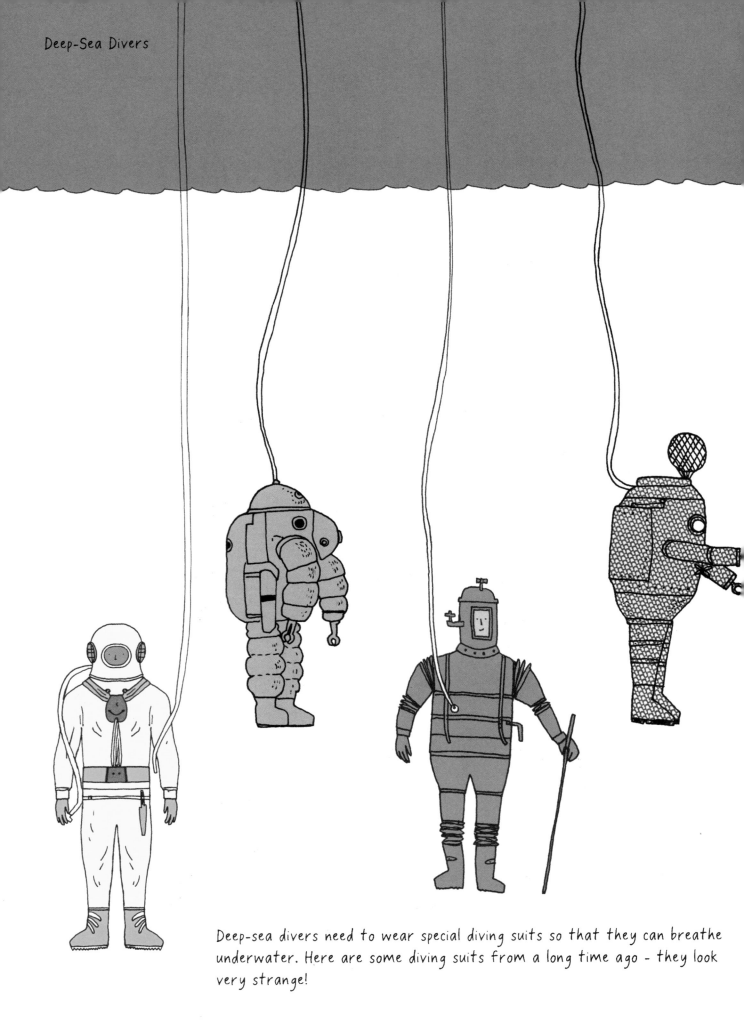

Deep-Sea Divers

Deep-sea divers need to wear special diving suits so that they can breathe underwater. Here are some diving suits from a long time ago - they look very strange!

Draw some more divers in the sea.

Latitude and Longitude

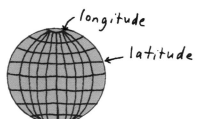

The world is divided by imaginary lines known as latitude and longitude. Lines of latitude run horizontally across the globe, while lines of longitude run vertically down it. These lines are helpful in pinpointing an exact spot on a map and can help sailors navigate while at sea.

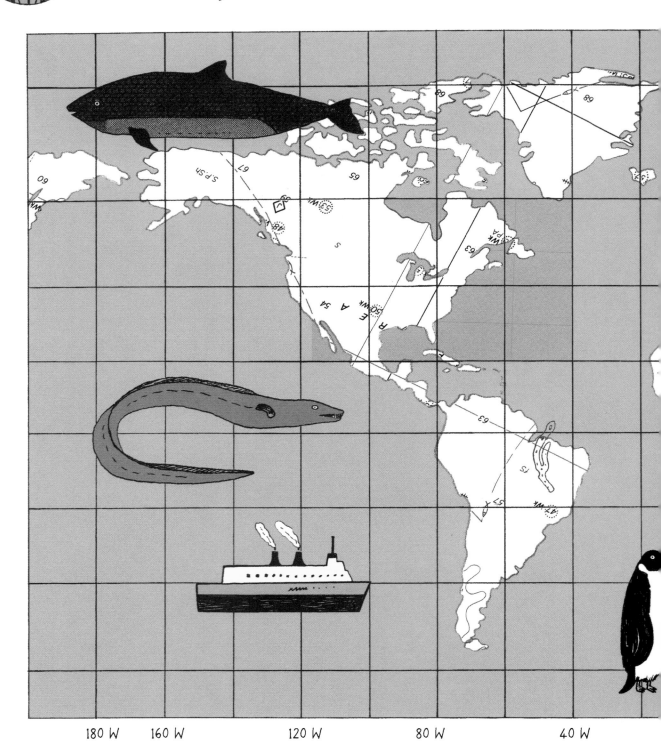

180 W   160 W   120 W   80 W   40 W

Draw a ship at 40 degrees west, 40 degrees north.

What can you see at 20 degrees west, 40 degrees south?

What can you see at 160 degrees east, 0 degrees?

Draw some buried treasure at 90 degrees east, 50 degrees north.

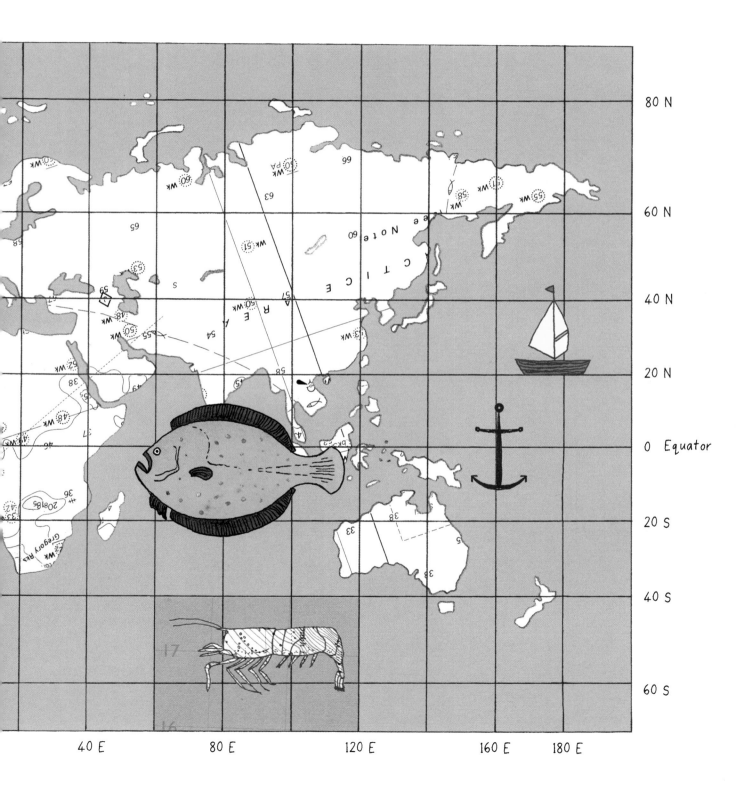

The Bermuda Triangle

The Bermuda Triangle is a triangle-shaped part of the North Atlantic Ocean where a number of planes and ships have mysteriously disappeared.

See if you can find two lost ships and three lost planes among the seaweed.

TIDES

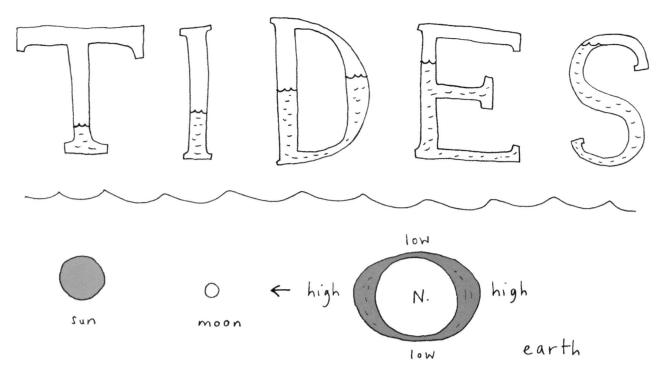

sun

moon

← high

low

N.

high

low

earth

Tides are great bulges of water caused by the gravity of the moon and sun. These bulges move around the earth as it spins, causing water levels to rise and fall. Typically, water will rise for about six hours and then start falling again.

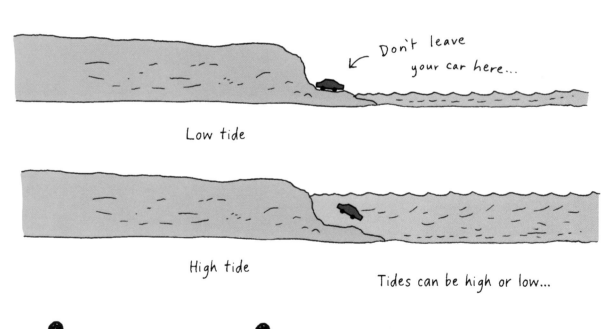

← Don't leave your car here...

Low tide

High tide

Tides can be high or low...

Low tide

High tide

Somewhere in the middle

Draw some other things at low and high tide...

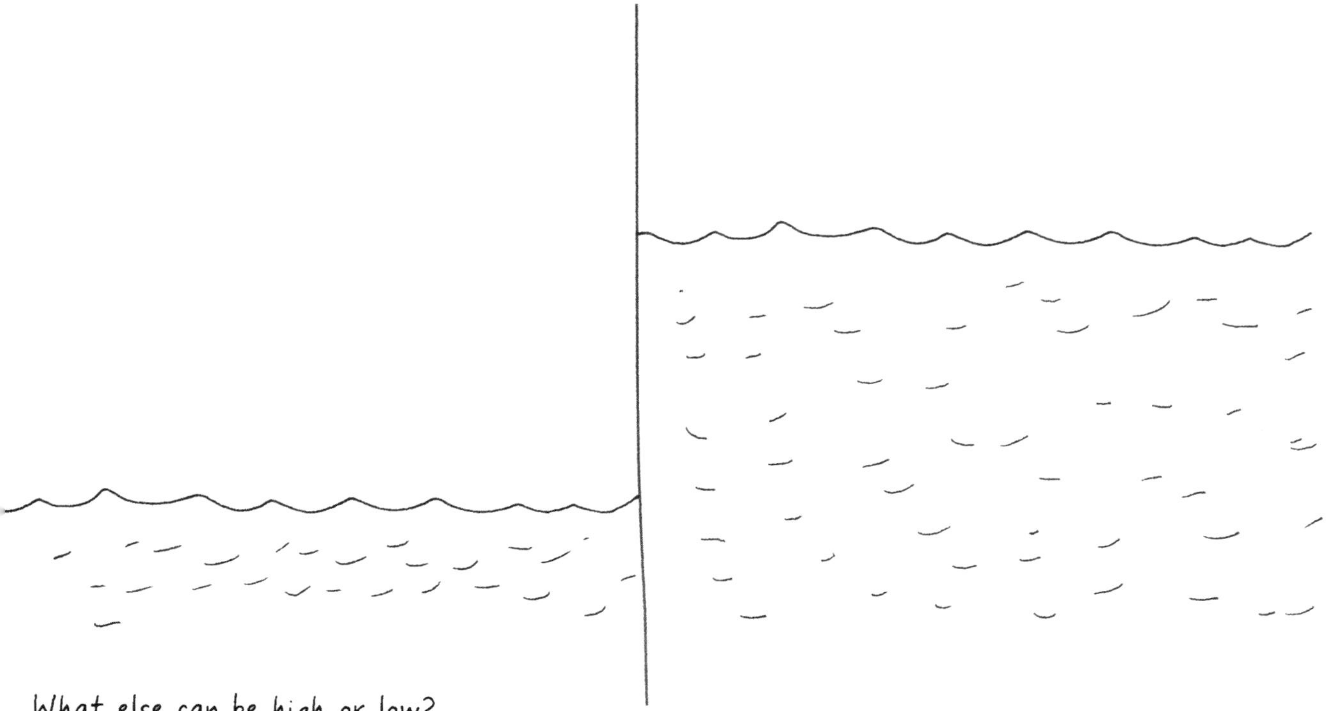

What else can be high or low?

high   low

Bangs

low   high

Cup of coffee

Can you think of some more?

7

6

5

4

3

2

1

Energy from the SEA

The sea is very important in providing a lot of the energy we use every day. Fossil fuels such as oil and gas are extracted from under the seabed using a very large drill.

Wind farms are often situated in the sea...

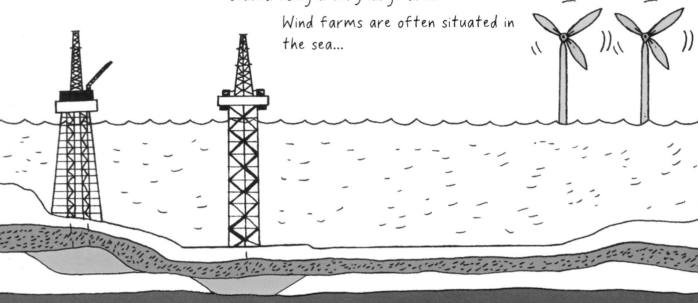

... and energy from the waves can also be used to provide energy. This is very good because it is renewable - it won't run out like oil and gas.

This house is using energy provided by the sea. Draw some things that use electricity inside the house.

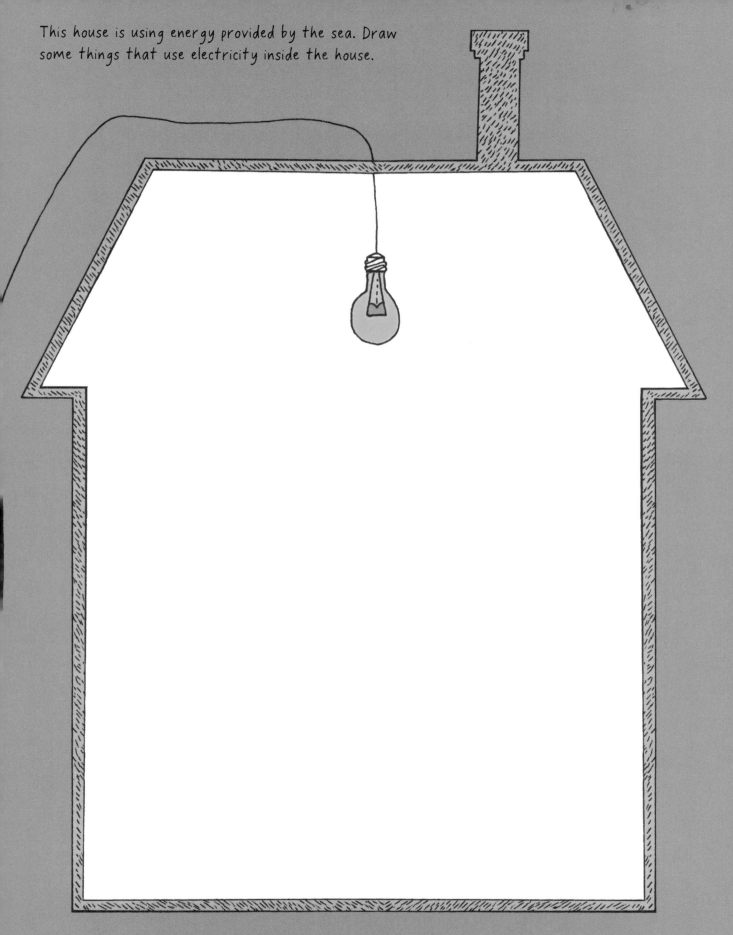

We need energy for heat and light, and to cook our food...

LOBSTER

What color is a lobster?

uncooked

aaargh

A lobster is blue-gray before it is cooked
and an orangey-red afterwards.
Color the uncooked lobster blue and the
cooked lobster red.

cooked

Seahorses

Seahorses have no teeth and no stomach. Food passes through their digestive system so quickly that they must eat almost constantly to stay alive.
They eat a balanced diet of brine shrimp, sausages, cake, and carrots.

Here are some hungry seahorses. Quick! Draw lots of food for them to eat!

But they do not often come by sausages, cake, and carrots, so usually just brine shrimp.

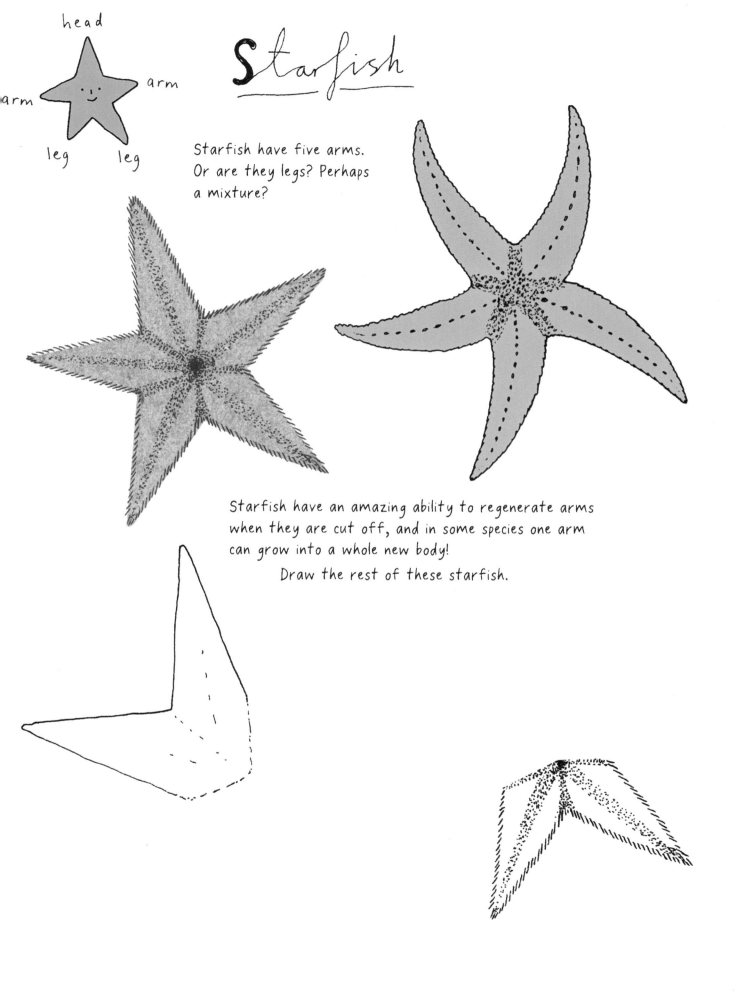

head

arm

arm

leg   leg

Starfish

Starfish have five arms.
Or are they legs? Perhaps
a mixture?

Starfish have an amazing ability to regenerate arms
when they are cut off, and in some species one arm
can grow into a whole new body!

Draw the rest of these starfish.

There are many stars in the sky, and there are many starfish on the beach!
The stars are arranged in patterns called constellations. Some of these are based on the signs of the zodiac.

Can you make up your own constellations using starfish?

Fantastic fish

Here are some strange-looking fish.
Make up some of your own!

Catfish

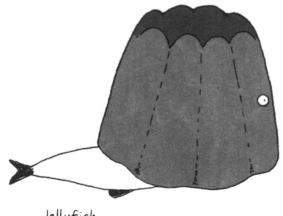

Jellyfish

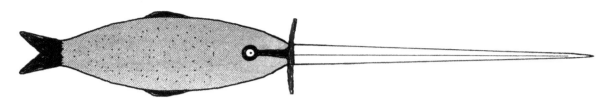

Swordfish

Dogfish

Whale Spouts

Whales are mammals and they cannot breathe underwater. They breathe through blowholes on the tops of their heads. When the whale breathes out, a spout of air and water vapor is expelled into the air. Draw spouts coming from these whales' blowholes.

pygmy
sperm whale

Make an **Origami boat**

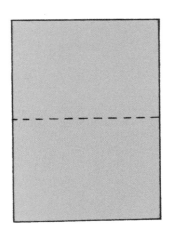

1   Start with a piece of paper, and fold it in half.

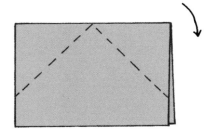

2

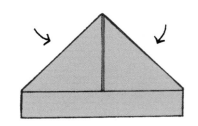

3   Fold the corners in.

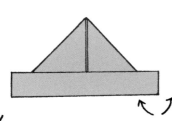

4   Fold the bottom edge to meet the bottom of the triangles. Repeat behind.

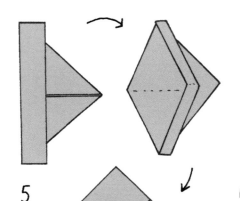

5

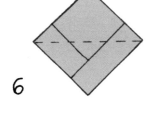

6

Lift the middle and pull outward. Push both points together and squash down. You should have a square.

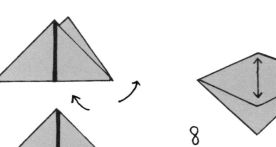

7   Fold bottom point upward so you have a triangle. Turn over and repeat.

8

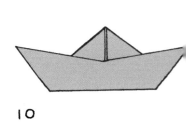

9

10

Now open and pull points outward and squash down to form the bottom of the boat.

Decorate your boat and give it a name!

Decorate these boats!

Plankton tales

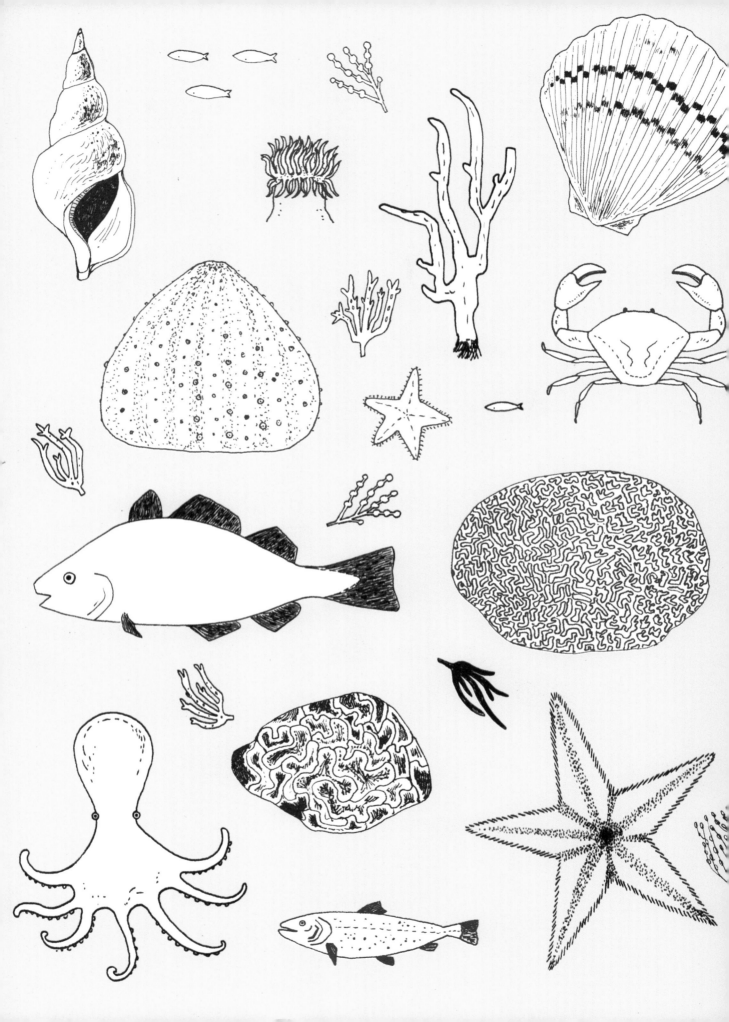